Charles Nelan

Cartoons of Our War with Spain

Charles Nelan

Cartoons of Our War with Spain

ISBN/EAN: 9783337245764

Printed in Europe, USA, Canada, Australia, Japan

Cover: Foto ©ninafisch / pixelio.de

More available books at **www.hansebooks.com**

CARTOONS OF OUR WAR WITH SPAIN

"A laugh is worth a hundred groans in any market."—LAMB.

Cartoons of our war with Spain.

By Ch. Nelan

FREDERICK A. STOKES COMPANY, PUBLISHERS, NEW YORK

Dedicated to The American People.

Very respectfully yours—

Chs. Nelan.

INTRODUCTION

MY publishers have asked me to write something. This I have already done on every page,—in the picture language, in which alone do I feel that I can do my best. Ten years ago an old German editor in my native State, Ohio, said, "The cartoon will be the editorial of the future."

In this day of American journalistic enterprise, the cartoonist is often called on to make a cartoon in two or three hours and sometimes in less time. Do you wonder that we die young or become paretics?

If we do anything towards moulding public opinion, do not blame us entirely, but remember the editor, whose name does not appear on the cartoon.

I do not believe in the bitter, stinging cartoon. It's always best to produce a laugh with your argument; people seem to digest it better.

I desire to acknowledge the courtesy of the NEW YORK HERALD in permitting me to publish these cartoons in book form.

CHARLES NELAN,
With the *New York Herald.*

KEEP YOUR HEAD COOL.

"MUST I GET OUT?"

DON'T BOTHER THE PILOT.

HE WOULDN'T BE HAPPY UNTIL HE GOT IT.

IT BEGINS TO LOOK AS IF THESE GENTLEMEN AGREED WITH ME

PEACE OR WAR?

"WHERE AM I AT?"

"APRIL FOOL!"

A "SHELLING" FOR UNCLE SAM'S EASTER MONDAY.

BEFORE AND AFTER TAKING—RESPONSIBILITY.

"WELL, I'M WAITING NOW."

A SNAP SHOT.

RALLY ROUND THE FLAG.

TAKING HIS PULSE.

BETWEEN TWO FIRES

THE PRESENT: TO THE STARS AND STRIPES DEWEY OPENED A NEW WORLD.

"DON'T SMILE TILL YOU HEAR FROM SAMPSON."

"WELL, WHO'LL BE NEXT?"

SPAIN'S DILEMMA.

ALL SIZES AND GOOD FITS FOR ALL THE FAMILY.

MANILA.

PORTO RICO.

SATISFYING SPANISH HONOUR.

NOTICE!

LOST, STRAYED OR STOLEN —
ONE CAPE VERDE FLEET!
Any one bringing it
to me will be rewar-
ded.

U. S.

INFORMATION WANTED.

SHE'S TUMBLING!

JUST MISSED!

COUSINS.

"WHAT ARE THE WILD WAVES SAYING?"

BOTTLED. WILL HE ESCAPE?

IF THE WAR BRING NOTHING ELSE, WE ARE THANKFUL.

IN
MEMORY
of
the HEROES
of
THE MAINE, SAN JUAN,
CARDENAS, CIENFUEGOS,
&c.

THEIR FIRST DECORATION DAY. KEEP THEIR GRAVES GREEN.

"THE CONCERT OF EUROPE."

THE KING'S JESTER

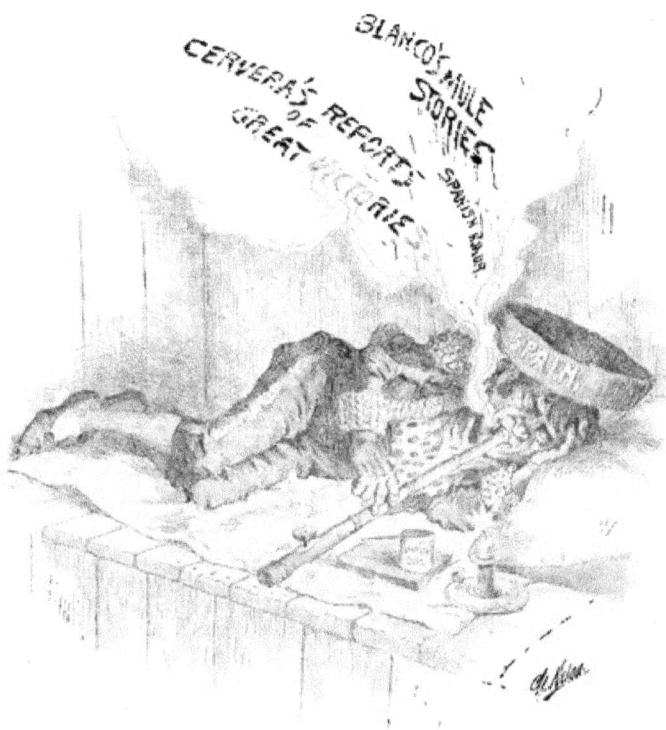

HOW WILL HE FEEL WHEN THE PIPE GIVES OUT?

AND THEN ALONG CAME THE REAL KING,

HE ISN'T HANDSOME, BUT HE COMES HIGH.

WILLIAM, YOU'RE TOO LATE.

U. S.: WELL, THE PATRIOTS ARE NOT ALL IN THE ARMY.

"I WONDER IF HE REALLY WANTS MY WHITE ELEPHANT."

GRAND
SUMMER
EXCURSION
TO SPAIN.
PYROTECNIC
DISPLAYS
AT BARCELONA, CADIZ
AND OTHER SPANISH COAST
BRING YOUR FIREWORKS AND
HAVE A GOOD TIME !

ANNOUNCEMENT EXTRAORDINARY.

TROUBLES WHICH MAY FOLLOW AN IMPERIAL POLICY.

"YOU'RE NEXT!"

THE BIRTH OF A MARINE GIANT.

"THE BOY STOOD ON THE BURNING DECK."

YOUR ONLY SALVATION.

BE CAREFUL.

NERO FIDDLED WHILE ROME BURNED.

EUROPE: "MY GOODNESS, HOW HE IS MUTILATING THAT BEAUTIFUL MAP!"

"GENTLEMEN, AS THE SPANIARD IN THE CAST IS BEHIND IN HIS LINES, THERE WILL
BE A SHORT INTERMISSION."

BEFORE AND AFTER TAKING. UNCLE SAM FREELY TELLS HIS PHYSICIAN THAT HIS
TREATMENT HAS BEEN A SUCCESS.

TWO THINGS HE HAS LEARNED.

UNCLE SAM PAYS THE FREIGHT.

THIS ISN'T TOO MUCH FOR A GOOD THING

THE END.

www.ingramcontent.com/pod-product-compliance
Lightning Source LLC
Chambersburg PA
CBHW021522090426
42739CB00007B/738